Dedication:

For my children Bruce, Jody, Lori, Jeff and Danny, all my grandchildren, and especially remembering Hu, Tommy, and Bruce and Ethel Farrell, my parents.

Twice in a Blue Moon

poems by Joyce Harries

...because once in a blue moon you get a first book published at the age of seventy-two, and maybe it can happen twice...

2007 © Joyce Harries

Published by Spotted Cow Press
4216 - 121 Street
Edmonton, Alberta
Canada T6J 1Y8
www.spottedcowpress.ca

First Printing

Library and Archives Canada Cataloguing in Publication

Harries, Joyce, 1928-
    Twice in a blue moon : poems / by Joyce Harries.

Issued also in electronic format.

ISBN 978-0-9780415-1-9

    I. Title.

PS8615.A7465T94 2007   C811'.6   C2007-905263-0

Printed and bound in Canada

Design and layout by Melanie Eastley, some production!

Distributed by Northwest Passages (www.nwpassages.com)

Twice in a Blue Moon

Acknowledgements:

My thanks to all who have helped me with this book of
poetry, including the generous quibblers in my three
writing groups, and those in the Edmonton Stroll of Poets'
Society who kept me listening. My teacher-mentors,
Jack Bilsland, Tim Bowling, Eunice Scarfe, Margaret
Macpherson and Shirley Service encouraged me to "keep
writing". And most of all my children and their families
who spur me on: Bruce, Karen, Stephanie and Lucas, Jody,
Bill, Tommy, Lori and Annie, Lori, Tasli and Kyli, Jeff, Noni,
Molly, Hu, Rosie, Katie, Angus, Maggie, Bruce, Emmett and
Annie and my son Danny, my co-editor. Also my thanks
to The Alberta Foundation for the Arts for making me
feel my writing is worthwhile, and to Jerome and Merle
Martin of Spotted Cow Press who took a chance.

Contents

Beginnings Again

What If

what if I could take a
hiatus
from aging
could pause the clock
linger at the age of choice

where would I stall?
at sixteen?
when I knew so little
thought I knew so much
World War II ended
boys
no particular thoughts of the future
not like
today's youth
who have to contend with
ecological disasters
and terrorists

would I stall
at thirty-two?
when the last of our
babies was born
we'd lost one child
but the other five were healthy and bright
my devoted husband at my side

would I stall
at fifty-two?
when I sweated through menopause easily
and life was good

would I stall
at my fifty-eighth birthday?
ignorant of my husband's impending death
in two weeks
because of course
if time stopped then
he wouldn't have
taken that last ride

would I stall
at seventy?
wink at father time
my good luck holding
after all
only seven years have passed
since then
though my eyes dim
and my feet
ache with arthritis
I rejoice, celebrate
even blossom occasionally

Twice in a Blue Moon

Beginnings

Oblivion

I once lived in
the dirty 30's
I did not know
our landlord
held back our rent
or about Dad's serious gambling
after all
he only did it
when the ponies were in town
at summer fairs
then he would party
with his pals and
bring me a pink and white stuffed dog
I called Sweetheart

In my land of oblivion
I did not realize how much my dad
loved my mother
while I watched
he would kiss and touch her
he never raised his voice to her
nor she to him
they never said I love you
out loud
that I heard

In that land
I didn't know
not really know
when the gin bottles and the canned grapefruit juice
sat on the kitchen table
my mother's face lengthened
my dad's smile widened
and I would go early to bed
with a book

In this land of oblivion
no brothers
no girlfriends or sisters
who knew of such things
as kissing
and groping
no beds, or making out on pool tables

then I learned what it was all about
I traveled a fast track
said "I do"
became wise to
what he liked
and what I liked
to birthing babies
juggling time
cooking for multitudes
tired tired
and finally burying a child

4

I knew my world
was full enough
as I partnered a kind and courtly man
and tried to advise our adolescents

later, he died
I still made chutneys
picked flowers
tomatoes
kept up with news, books
theatre, fashion, foods

talked to the public
   told it all
     nearly all

The Contortionist

I'd never heard that word
though friends called me rubber legs
so long ago
birthday parties
little girls in peach or blue taffeta
ruffles at knees and neck
white ankle socks
black patent leather shoes
after pin-the-tail-on-the-donkey
the farmer-in-the-dell
and musical chairs
the talent show
There is a Tavern in the Town in the town
the highway man came riding riding riding
perfect performances
much clapping
my turn
like a stork on one leg
the other twined around my neck
I hopped the length of the living room
my finale
both legs around my neck
a friend pushed
and I somersaulted into
short-lived fame

MacIntosh Toffee, Circa 1935

a small red box slashed with tartan

inside crisp wax paper

held a golden slab

I cracked on a bicycle handle

its hard shards shared we held the pieces in our mouths

savoring sugar sweetness

melted butter mass softened

rolled over our tongues

stuck our teeth together

we giggled

breathed through our noses

'til the golden cement

ceased to exist

except in our memories

Seduced

His words poured like silk-velvet
popped like mustard seeds in a hot skillet
thunked like a shovel in gumbo
rat-tatted like a drummer in a school-boys' band
spurted like crushed pomegranate seeds
sprinkled and melted like brown sugar on oatmeal porridge
fluttered like a venetian blind in an open window
hooted like a train whistle
and lullabyed

she was lost

Fred Astaire and Me

I have a friend who
dances with Gene Kelly
not me
too athletic less graceful than
Fred Astaire
my partner
I don't want to splish splash in the rain
although I do love that song

I want a swirling ball gown
smaller feet than I possess
in strappy sandals
and long swinging blond hair
and a name as peppy as Ginger
not Joyce

he will twirl me in a garden
its flagstones smooth
and we will float on lily pads
till we come to a bridge
we magically fly over

when I change my clothes
to wide white shorts and top
and meet Fred on the stairs
we will click our way

up and down and partly up
and partly down and two at a time
and backwards without a glance

and we will dance to mirrors
four of us
two Freds and two Allspices
if that's what I become

I like Fred best
the calm   in-control way
he partners
Gene is all for Gene
and should dance alone
Fred makes even me
look good

Middles

Yugoslavia September, 1972

if I just think hard enough
I can hear
that creaking too-short bed in
that Yugoslavian pension on
that bay
near the top of the Adriatic
on that morning
when we woke
he laughed
at the plastic sheet crumpled
under damp linen

if I just think hard enough
I can taste
that night before
warm
laden fig tree at the open window
my nightie on the floor

if I just think hard enough
I can almost   but not quite
feel that feeling
hear him
breathing my name

That Time

that time
we drove to Banff
through swirling snow
which way was down or up
I didn't know
I was dizzy
a co-pilot without maps
you drove as if through
clouds of dust in pastures
windshield wipers flopped
we both squinted
at black speckled whiteness
could your long distance eyes
see into the future

Endings

Sometimes You Don't Need the Words

I had never heard him say
I love you
but I knew he did

I felt him standing quietly
at my bedroom door
when I was feverish
and when my eyes closed
his cool hand rubbed my back
until I fell asleep

I sensed his sadness when I was naughty and Mummy scolded me

In 1939 I spat out sucked pomegranate seeds
from exotic hard-shelled
pink globes he bought for me at a Chinese grocery store
in the days when *I love you* was saved for sweethearts and valentines
not for children

I knew it when I wavered on my red two-wheeler
his hand holding onto the seat
his puffing encouragement
his legs flailing
his laughing when I wobbled alone
down the straight cinder road

my blond curls bouncing
my little hands gripping red rubber
my scabbed knees bending and straightening
bending and straightening

I knew it when we smoked cigarettes
together on the backyard canvas swing
he listened to my chatter and I knew
though he never said it

He was so polite and soft-spoken
an aunt told me *He bumped into my canary's cage and said*
Excuse me

When I became old, a friend told me what I had forgotten
that he came home when my friends were at play
and hugged me and said *Hi princess. Hello girls*
I knew it then

I knew it when I held his hand in the hospital
one useless hand
limp on the white cover
his good hand clutching mine
as he had my bicycle seat
so long ago
unable to say the words

I had never needed to hear

At the Hospital

she smiled
eyes bright unknowing
pink and white dotted scarf
askew on bald head
bed-jacket's lace yellow and old
I told her remember
our tea parties
the oilcloth placemat you painted
with the little red hen and the black rooster
you knit my blue sweater with flowers and tassels
made divinity fudge that Peter Pug ate
when we made Christmas cakes you let me cut the cherries
and when I asked about boys – you laughed and said
kid them along

I rubbed her legs
the same age mine are now
fed her soup jello
said It won't be long
asked her doctor
what he would do
if it were his mother

keep her comfortable
and love her

they did

I did

and away she went

Did He Know?

arena dirt scuffled and lumped under
his hooves
sun blazing
trough water lukewarm
bleachers full of spectators
horse trailer chrome too hot to touch
heat haze

his name
Doc's Twister
did he have some
slight medical knowledge
a sire's wisdom
passed down to know
a rider's every nuance

what did he think
could he have known the reason
why his rider was pulled from his back
after their ride together
when young steers huffed and deeked
from side to side wild eyed and confused

did he sense something wrong
were the secret signals of rider to horse
muffled by a heart sputtering to stillness

jumping nervously muscles still quivering
from their ride together
neck glistening where his rider
had placed a hand to signal
stop
then a change
dead weight flopped over saddle horn
other riders closed in
weight pulled from his back
led prancing away
to be walked 'round and 'round and 'round
as though the walker was in a daze

did he know
did he shake his head
did he eat his oats
did he grieve

Answering Sappho

it's private
but believe me
the first time was first

he fell asleep after
but I didn't

barefoot I looked
down at him
and smiled

Aphrodite
we are on the same
wave length

and I said
I will cook
for you all your life

we danced at balls
and in the kitchen
jazz from the radio thrumming

when I was roundest
we went to the hospital
and lo and behold
another blond almost bald baby

I confess you taught
me more than I taught you
you are still in the sun's rays

at bedtime
the moon looks for you
a cat howls
one side of the bed is empty

I cannot carry a tune
but your voice sings
for us two
and lulls me to sleep

these words are silent
but float somewhere to you
I was so young
you weren't

I'm a slow learner
now I know what I've lost

I will not beat my breasts calling
"my Adonis is dead"
he lives on

it's no use friends
you cannot find me
another mate
nor do I want one

I know people talk
wondering why I smile
in my singleness

I have ceased recently
drinking scotch before
solitary dinners
why is this

Eros tells me
keep going old girl
and folds his wings around me

please Hesperus
show him the trail
he may gallop on Twister

in my dreams you wear two hats
a Stetson
and a tasseled mortarboard

as the August moon shines
wife, children and grandchildren
make a circle around your spirit

Persephone took the
dust you became
placing it with our son
would you rather we
had flung it to the winds

Ashes to Diamonds

ah
the diamond ring
on my finger
what if it were twinned
with a diamond
from different ashes
this time the
remains of that lovely man
who placed my first ring
fifty-four years ago
when I was innocent

rather than ashes nestled
in our small son's grave
Hu would turn to diamond
keep me company
shower and sleep with me
hug our children
hold our grandchildren

die with me

Holding Hands

he shuffles she takes short quick steps
he needs a neck trim the seat of her slacks is droopy
I walk behind them impatiently
but notice their hands are clasped
and I think of my long gone man
who held my hand when first we blind-dated
to a movie at the Capitol theatre

when we walked the hospital corridor
to the viewing window of the maternity nursery
we held hands while gazing at our first child
and our second, our third,
our fourth, our fifth, and our sixth

when we walked to the rink to see our children skate
the back lane icy he held my hand

he held my hand when we followed our eldest son's coffin,
the sky gray and low

and when we walked that last hill together
Okanagan dust puffed 'round our feet
we swung clasped hands
looked up the mountain
heat hazed and hot

his hand large though fingers clever
enough to fix a watch write a speech or essay

and I wonder if he were still alive
would we two be holding hands
shuffling and quick stepping down the avenue
an impatient widow on our heels

Life's Cruelties

An old man questions the perky cashier

asks how many airmiles

a package of pork liver one loaf of white bread and three onions

will give him

you see he has his reasons

it takes so long to save enough points to visit his grandchildren

who are never brought to visit him

he picks up his fallen cane

adjusts his black-banded straw hat

grabs his double bagged purchase

turns to the waiting line

their baskets bulging with diet coke potato chips light cuisine TV dinners

waves and says "have a nice day"

totters across the parking lot

where he is hit by a car driven by a woman who has just had a stroke

And Goings On

Steam on a Bathroom Mirror

steam on a mirror
hides lines
    creases
    folds and
years of inner tears

she draws a heart
swipes its center
sees with fading sight
what once was smooth and
    smiling

sucks in moist breath
gets dressed and
    carries on

How to Leave Mothering

You can't
when all of a sudden
your children age
you've stopped buying
baby powder pablum diapers
you've stopped folding piles of bluejeans
and listening for teenage nighttime footsteps

Bite your tongue
you can't say you forgot your mittens your homework your manners

Only think of the sweet smell of a tiny baby fresh bathed pajama-clad bodies
reading aloud giggles from tickling goodnight kisses
think of a door bursting open "I'm home I've brought a friend any cookies?"
think of their glowing faces after they jumped in a jolly jumper first drank
through a straw printed their name hammered a nail skipped bounced a ball
played Twinkle Twinkle Little Star on the piano rode a wobbling two-wheeler
watched fireworks made rice krispie squares put a pony over a jump emerged
from puberty played old maid monopoly poker got their driver's licence went
on their first date graduated from high school from university married gave
you grandchildren

Quote anything correctly to them shorten your stories don't talk about *your*
life unless you've been robbed taken to the hospital won a lottery or award
preface statements with "dear"

Think about Christmas when they were young how tired you were bite your
tongue in daughters' or sons' kitchens where turkey is still turkey on someone
else's platter

Think of those late night talks at the kitchen table with tea and cookies when *they* asked *your* advice now *they* dispense it bite your tongue smile and thank them

Remember measles chicken-pox band aids crutches vomit diarrhea earaches hospital emergency line ups but remember rocking humming stroking patting laughter joy

You still can visit give them jars of homemade soup marmalade flowers and books
 worry about them   love them their spouses and children

and bite your tongue

Reprinted with permission. Originally published in the Journal of the Association for Research in Mothering, Spring/Summer 2003, Volume 5, #1, York University (Toronto, Canada)

Crumbs Fall Where They May

if crumbs fall where they may
if kindness crumbs are small
    meet eyes at grocery store
    let a car go in front
    say I know, I know, and do
if crumbs are deep blue mould
    no letter
    no call
    no crumb

if ice patches sidewalks
    knees and hips complain
    deep breaths in
    deep breaths out

if last mock orange leaves cling
    sky low
    gray
    magpie skitters in roof gutter
    pretend fireplace log spews
    cobalt blue

    she reads by east window
    morning light washes her book

    thinks off the pages
    longing to replay her life
    with crumbs of what she now knows

If I Could Choose Again

if I could choose again
at the start
the starting gate
the beginning
I would choose
what chose me
the parents
the husband
the children
purple earrings
ease in kitchens
pleasure with words
I'd watch carefully
bide my time
speak softly
to a tomato
growing large and fragrant
on my east patio
prop up
my aching heart
with bridal bouquets
of lilies orchids
and roses

A Bra Story for Seniors

what's new   we said
she winked   dropped a shoulder
unbuttoned blouse top
not *a* bra
    the bra
over iced lattes shrimp salad with blood oranges
we stared   envious
thinking of our own   old lady whites
under-wired like winter tires
hers   non skid straps of
pink coral and yellow daisies
overlapping circles of same supported two
proud possessions
I'll impress a granddaughter she said
where's the thong   we asked
sarong you say
    why would I need that

Keep Dancing

I remember thinking
doesn't she know
doesn't she know

her mouth a scarlet slash
two red circled cheeks
dyed red split-ended hair

long silver earrings tinkle
stars and moonbeams down
her wrinkled neck

stubborn chicken bones in a tight black leotard
she places mishapen feet
precisely
without thinking

her hands red talloned blue veined and knarled
wave in time to the music
she calls

that's it
that's it
keep it up
keep it up
never stop
keep going
keep going
you're beautiful

keep dancing
keep dancing

A Busybody Transplants Poppies

They didn't all transplant. Those grey-green half inch high oriental poppy plants.

Stubborn most of them were. I'd read they liked to start from seed and hated being moved to strange places but you see I had these pots – ones I couldn't afford to fill
with geraniums or petunias so I figured it was worth a try. Crowded together they looked up at me. Some brave and adventurous. Some drooped and turned yellow. Black earth showed. If I picked them for my kitchen table their stems would have to be seared.

And people walked past laughing while their dogs sniffed tree trunks. A helicopter flew overhead on its way to the hospital. Leaves dislodged and fluttered to my feet. What's for dinner? Should I feed poppies 20-20-20 or only water? That man getting out of the blue car looks like somebody.

A Slow Day

they write and they write and they write
fingers twitter on laptops
they smile
a teardrop slides
tree branches glisten
clouds roll by
the sky turns bluer

her pen jerks
pauses in mid-air
she mouths words
like grocery lists
days on her calendar
but not
flowing phantoms of memories
when she was ripe
every bud bursting
laughter with dessert

today her head spacey
from too little sleep
a shame
last day
for concentration 101

A Wandering Mind

a wandering mind walks
not along a river valley trail
but alongside puffing diesel buses
sides painted over   windows included
can't believe passengers can see through
do I look striped like the tiger grinning
at a sleek new car or
do dazzling giant white teeth appear on my forehead
is a coke can balanced on my shoulder or
does a ferocious football hero march beside me
do these people on the bus wonder why I'm walking instead of riding
wonder at my blowing white hair

if I could see their faces
I would look for a glimmer of a smile when a woman thinks of her child
home first   setting the table   turning on the potatoes   the porch light
filling the dog's water bowl tearing salad lettuce and reading an essay for tomorrow
and I would look for a man's face looking out   his lips drawn tight
thinks he must break the downsizing news   stop wasting bus tickets
when the job finished last Tuesday
and anyway she's still working   or is she
and the student   so young   she must be
her head down   probably a book on her lap
an Annie Leibowitz profile   though less well lit
on her way to her five to midnight job
taking care of an elderly Alzheimer man
family can't agree on where to send him
she might be able to finish her math assignment

though he has days and nights mixed
last night lunged his frail frame at her while on his way to catch the last train
for Ottawa   he said

at the bus stop I slow my healthy pace
try not to breath diesel fumes deeply
watch a woman no older than me
hobble with the aid of a much too short cane
to the bus   her face grimaces   needs a Tylenol
her purse strap slides from shoulder to inner elbow   dangles at ankle height
unbalancing her so she staggers against the bus's open door
the driver lunges for her   rights her like a Russian doll
she disappears from my view

it's one thing to walk the valley
hear birds   animal rustlings
breathe deep the fragrant air
I'm not against nature
but where does my mind wander then
to mystery theatre bodies buried on a bluff
or lovers beyond that copse letters carved on a sturdy tree   carver long dead
or the first wood violets of spring
a hermit's long-ago cave
and what happened to him anyway
a cyclist streaks past   shaved legs glisten   Gatorade tilts to lips
perhaps a recovered heart patient
a man knows in years he's past his prime   but won't admit it

a wandering mind can travel at a table
blank sheet waits for words to spew

jerk spew halt flow dribble drip drip stop

About What People Think

how much do I really care
less than when I was young
I've flopped over that fence
not too gracefully
where blurting a thought
and meeting raised eyebrows
does not leave me mortified
and red in the face
I'm old enough to know
they too have made mistakes
they too have silly ideas
in their DNA's

Admit It

senior moments when
my brain stalls
a name
a word
a concept
disappears
in the mists of my mind

I rationalize
surely when I was young
I forgot library books
assignment dates
date of my period
cousin's birthdays

I worry
I see in friends' eyes
a sliding nothing
bewilderment
their clever cover-ups

they are the same
only different

am I too

My Mind a Closet

new brooms sweep clean
ring out the old
ring in the new
clean my closet or clean my clock
dusty thoughts from back corners
sort throw
sort throw
ideas are missing socks
half there
crooked hangers
meant to be useful
thwarted when twisted
a sagging pole
holds too much
a tilting shelf
threatens
scarves memories socks purses
summer t-shirts
love letters
condolence letters   spill
onto suit-cased backpacked shoe-laden floor
louvered doors close when a kick
moves debris back
all looks serene
but is it

And Still They Grow

side by side we walked new Paradise roads
beige talcum powder
puffed with every step
we sprinkled wild grass seeds
from apple pickers' bags
along steep and twisted cliffs
avalanches waiting to happen

our seeds held their breath
till snow melt and spring rain
pushed tough threads
past sage brush, bear and coyote dung
green ends nobbed with buds of May
pink bumps burst into blossom
waved and shimmered in Okanagan heat

year after year after year
the cliffs hold

grasses grow and blow

of the two who sowed
only I am here to see success

One More Word

if I hear one more word

about once you hit seventy

it's all downhill

as though at midnight of that birthday

a switch clicks

and each body system turns to one another and says

you first   I'll take my turn

and one at a time

hip joints seize

knees creak

arteries clog

earlobes lengthen

hair thins

nose drips

face lines deepen

eyebrow hairs turn wiry

gastric juices erupt

teeth crack

corneas wobble

pupils wrinkle

eyes dim

names elude memory

if I hear one more advising word
about the pills
try ginkgo biloba
vitamin E, Lutein and glucosamine
what about coenzyme Q10, bilberry
eat sardines weekly
don't drink coffee after noon
or go in the sun to pick nasturtiums unless you wear sunblock
and who do you think you are
painting your living room chartreuse when everyone else's is off-white
did you start wearing red when your husband died

if I hear one more teasing word
about grandchildren's pictures
floating from piles in purses
at lunch they're passed 'round like birthday cards
and the young waitress rolls her eyes when we divide the bill
hoping our tip will be generous enough
we've had our decaff skim lattes
our salads and no desserts thanks

and if I hear one more word
about how bad it is to age
I will throttle that person
probably a man
who can't flow with life's pattern
needs to stay young
marry dot com executive
has new family

silly old goat
why didn't he do it
right the first time

if I hear one more envious word
about that contemporary of ours
you know the one who runs with a pack of runners
the one who climbs mountains
boyfriends in three cities
skin taut
teeth white
hit a hole in one
can drink most men under the table

if I hear one more word about
some other women who are aberrations
who don't age
do they secretly spend one day a week in bed
like titled English authors once did
and bathe in chamomile or sea salt
have private masseuses
silk undergarments between lavender sachets
bed-sheets slippery satin
bedrooms overlooking parks
morning tea tray holding yellow roses

if I hear one more aging comment
I will reply reasonably
        prolonging my prime of life

yes
some of what you say is true

but oh
        to wake   stretch   hear birdsong
        creak out of bed
        look in the mirror

yes   I'm still here

        bring in the paper
        put on the kettle
        whole wheat bread in toaster
        slather marmalade

embrace the day

Thanks Anyway

please don't surprise me
change my house
to suit your tastes
plaster over my plain walls
with gilt chips mixed in varnish
spread like icing in stripes exactly
two and one half inches wide
replace my down-filled chintz sofa
its dips and protuberances
matching my own
with a clean-lined hard cored
fuzzy fabric wrapped item
uninviting as mossy mountain boulders

oh I know you call it
editing possessions
and you would edit pictures
of seventeen grandchildren on two tables somehow
into properly matted same size frames
on a focus wall   but then
where would my large acrylic of our old ranch gate and
the watercolors looking out the window down the lake to Penticton go
your choices would not be mine

thanks anyway but please don't re-sort my kitchen
to suit your ways
you'd put silver in a drawer next to the sink
I want it next to the table
you'd sort my catch-all drawer
eliminate my water pics
and where would my artificial fruit filled bowl
be without fresh flowers in its midst
four different scissors
for clipping newspaper, chives, zip bag tops or scalloped labels for marmalade
marking pens, black and gold to address grandchildren's birthday gifts
you'd do away with half sprouted bulbs – late - intended for Christmas
in February I can use a touch of red
then when long green leaves
started to droop
you'd throw them in the garbage
while I let them languish
under the kitchen bench
till spring when they go outside

you'd remove my old rolling secretarial chairs
substitute clean-lined Ikea's
and I'd lose their hard-to-change
slipcovers made with unbleached cotton once
curtains at Hidden Bar Ranch
and when I have more guests than for six mahogany chairs
these roll into place like
good little soldiers

and when you glimpse my den's couch
you'll say   whoa baby – how old is this
only fifty-six well worn years, two re-coverings and five slip-coverings
from original gray mohair to now blue and white shrunken
striped ticking, its welting worn,

even if you send me on a four-day spa weekend
I wouldn't thank you for your
underhanded work
and if you filmed me on return
I would surprise those in TV land and you too

with snarls and clenched teeth

Questions, Questions

I once was approached by a man
who thought
since I'd been introduced as an author
I was all-knowing
you know – an academic like him
who asked me questions
Shakespearian, mythological, operatic,
mathematical and religious

which I failed to answer
every single one

I could tell
he gave me a D minus

if he had asked

could I string a kind sentence
did I once know love
do I serenade with homemade soup
can I cook a chartreuse soufflé
or make a bride's bouquet

I would have passed his tests

The Chinese Visitor

a non English speaking math professor
from China is living at my house
and I'm English unilingual
we mostly talk on paper

he smiles at everything I say
as when I tell him
how to use a knife and fork with
French toast and maple syrup

he gifts me with bags of green tea
chunks of dehydrated mushrooms
chopsticks peanuts leather boxes
intricate red corded weavings
and purple satin somethings
his wife sent me cloisonné
bracelets and he cooked
twelve vegetable meals
sweat dripping from his
brow on chicken five-ways and
lemongrass

I sent his wife and daughter
tapes of me telling about my life
before and during *Jishou*
I took him to a farmer's market

where he bought maple sugar candy
and flower seeds

yesterday for two hours
at my breakfast table
laptop between us
flashing important lecture notes
I wore my editor's hat
wrote down changes
we laughed when I explained
repulsive numbers

this morning his note read
Thank you for your help
I can report my paper bravely

Zephyrs of Fear

still it happens
men at one end
women at the other
not as though they cannot
speak one another's language
although you might
think that is the case
the women outnumbering the men
hold their glasses
of red or white
since they have rolled
into that over seventy-five state
where canes hearing aids
eye surgeries and other signs
show topics will not be
diapers or pregnancy stories
they do not talk of hours
in meetings or cohorts on the shuttle
or their latest running times
it is more often about absent friends' trials
or deaths
or grandchildren's awards
fear in the world, or bargains on chicken thighs
these women have raised their families
not that they don't have concerns still
"small child small worry big child big worry"

at the other end of the room
what are the men laughing at
leaning back in chairs
eyes squinting shut
grasping hi-balls in cutglass
scotch not Mike's Hard Lemonade
are they talking about the past or
are they shaking their heads
and lowering their eyes
one more comrade
has hit the dust

the hostess tries to mix them up
like vinaigrette
three parts oil to one part vinegar
not that women are oily and men sour
but you know what I mean
it's the proportion in this age group
I used to read the birth announcements
now I read obits
marking my calendar with the
next funeral date and time
I turn to my notepaper
and tell yet one more widow
what she probably can't believe
that some day she will smile not cry
when she thinks of her husband

and those remaining men
you'd think they'd be proud
to be roosters in the clucking hen-house or
are they nervous looking over their shoulder
tiny zephyrs of fear blowing
who's next

An eBay Sale

I'm not kidding

when you trod on dusty window sills
pushed blinds inwards
so peeping Toms could see into
my inner sanctum

you sharpened your claws
on my precious leather covered swivel eBay chair
perfect back support for computer geeks the ad said
what once was butter smooth
now has your scratch marks

when you galloped
yes galloped   on new wooden floors
at four in the morning
your steps woke me from a dream
about my husband   which I don't have often enough
on return I couldn't pick up the complex story
which is your fault

you drank from the open toilet
licked your paws
jumped on the kitchen counter and caught a fly
stepped next to my head
claws tangled my tossed hair

you gaze at me
eyes yellow rounds
selfish thoughts
not like the
dog of the house
who knows my moods
smiles and wags his tail

sorry
that's why
I'm selling you on eBay

George

I could throw away all my other rooms tuck a bed
perhaps in a corner of my kitchen I would live
with bulbs of garlic shedding tissue skins
bananas speckling magazines and books
and clippings Indian cushions rollers on my chair
and a parrot on my ceiling
up near where I store the copper chafing dish
the too tall bottle of mulberry vinegar from 1985
when I shook a tree and the fruit fell onto a sheet
and the end result gave me a vinegar mother
which I haven't had one single minute in these past
twenty-one years to do anything about
this parrot will be perfect
not a papier-mâché one on a perch staring glassily
but a real talkin' swearin' breathin' croakin'
good-natured character it will be a "he"
I'm into guys in my kitchen they come up from
the basement read the morning papers with me drink
orange juice eat fruit with yogurt and granola slurp tea
they tell me of their life in academia
of which I know naught but I do get their faint drift
then they bring their rice cooker up at night it jiggles
they make curry and give me a taste

my parrot will be called George

Walking to the Beat

I stride down the street
reeboks thump
knees creak
hips groan
eyes squeeze
against a low September sun

hard hatted men
do not whistle at me

but hammer
to the beat of
I-don't-know-what
banga banga banga banga banga
banga bang

can't match my stride
to their too-loud
they-think- it's -music

the bobcat driver
twirls his machine
lifts the clay to a red truck box
thumpa thumpa thumpa thumpa thumpa
thumpa thump

goes my heart

The Ghostsniffer of My Mind

I smell a landfill

then turn to
raindrenched grass
a baby's neck after sleep
a meadow of fresh mown hay
sheets on a line
a tackroom with polished saddles
fallen autumn leaves

I smell flowers rotting in a vase

then turn to
bridal bouquets of freesia and roses
fresh cut Christmas trees
lilacs under a bedroom window
lily of the valley edging a path
sweet peas on a frost fence
sachets of lavender between sheets

I smell burnt toast

then turn to
coffee brewing
roasting Thanksgiving turkey

chocolate chip cookies on cooling racks
vanilla bean in hot milk
curried leftover lamb
cinnamon in applesauce

The ghostsniffer of my mind
works her craft
as do professional noses

 I sniff
aromatic memories
   my own aromatherapy

The Book Sale

from the bazaar's book table
Love, Sex and Aging
walked out the door
under the arm of a grizzled old man

is it wishful thinking
or practical points he needs

another man says
you should see his woman
she's a wow

good for you I think
wonder what other night tables
this book has seen

I sort the stacks
keep my eyes open
for like books
and twinkle-eyed men

Poetry in a Tea Lounge

I listened to a poet
his fans   sweet faced
giggling young women

especially one

he read of
wanting a lover

I understood   her glazed look
more reason
than fans at rock concerts
waving arms   through sweet smoke

she sat still perfectly still
tea cup cold
imagined his quest for her
her longing for him
is she a poet too

I thought of doe-eyed devotees
of Ted Hughes
wondered if   somehow
like Sylvia
this sensitive admirer
would connect
with black garbed poet
and live

happily   ever   after

The Witness

it's a matter of eyes, he claimed
well, how close did the witness get
he said they were blue as cornflowers
three of the jury members said no
but knew no botany
thought her eyes yellow like corn on the cob
from last nights barbecue
so that led them to argue in
their sequestered room about
cat's eyes yellow and gleaming
and they created the young woman's
character as a horse of a different colour
her true love had never known

did the woman blink those corncob eyes at her attacker
while beseeching the witness
do something do something
and really could he have been that close
to see terror turning
hazel eyes blue

M.S. and My Daughter Lori

if she could will them
to move
she would

tries
but
short circuit sparks
sputter fade
ashes blot movement
fire in her nerves
as from treetops
jump
sometimes to toes
cold and blue or
a bladder
contents now bagged in plastic

she laughs
when her wheelchair
clips door jams
plaster and paint fall

breadcrumbs in a forest
of mountains to climb

The Critic

shred it he said
shred it

you sound
like someone you're not
and Dad – he wasn't a failure
you sound like
a widow of the confederacy
the melodrama you paint
we didn't live
in the little house on the prairie

pretty tough stuff

how could a son
take such a slant
from my writing
are my memories only blue
is my poetic license
over the top

how could he think
I thought my husband a failure
that beautiful man who gave me
children like him

She's on My Side

She's my kindred spirit
that woman who sees
pink snapdragons and Chinese lanterns
and adds crabapple branches
She understands -
that woman who grins
when I hold hypericum berries next to peach roses
and talk of a bride in cream silk
She understands -
that woman who trusts
my taste since after all
it's like her own
and does not sniff
when I say enough red carnations
clumped together
can be Christmas
She listens
when I tell of unsettling
encounters with my children
and asks only the right questions
She doesn't change the subject
until I have run out of steam
when we once again
wade in petals and perfume
and I reconcile myself
to helplessness
as I float in flowers

Umbrellas

When I heard of the woman who married the man who made umbrellas I thought what was it about him? His choice of career? Or his desire to be useful or environmentally correct or artistic? Did his umbrellas shade babies in carriages or topless overheated bodies on beaches at Ipenema? Or were his umbrellas painted red poppies catching raindrops in Paris or did they appear on stage twirling in the rain tapping feet splashing melodies? Or were they precious parasols shading skin so white over lace and bustles and masterpiece theatre or bamboo parchment parasols on Thailand waterways grinning women selling melons and chickens? Or were lines of his umbrellas over black garbed nuns? Black skies. Black, black, black And did the woman who wished to marry the man who made umbrellas think his job so noble, so pure, they must be together? Wedding performed under canopy of white umbrellas beneath cloudless sky.

The Poet

She thinks she is working now
delphinium petals drop silently on kitchen table
she flips scribbler pages dates top line
let the words come let the words come
phone rings timer buzzes for laundry change
more petals drop

she writes
Aging brings inflexibility unless one is careful
not poetic wonders
if this affliction has hit her as it has some compatriots
her past drips with changed plans
different incomes—she preferred high
dreams of dancing shakes off sadness
turn off lights before Charlie Rose

try to like
sushi rising with the dawn grandchildren's music pierced navels
less butter and salt updating anti-virus programs

petals drop pick more add nasturtiums

let the words come let the words come

Life's Lottery

In a dark green room
not a theatre's green-room
a footstool holds misery-bunioned feet
Tiffany lamp over left shoulder
moonlight and sunlight
on linen snapped in silver hoops
crimson, aqua, daffodil, caviar black
silk embroidery floss
flows in miniature mounds
French knots, turkey work,
satin stitch and herringbone
Her needle comments on that long
scandalous life
where she was not sensible
responsible or
dependable
She had been so glamorous
so joyous
Her famous face
on fan magazine covers
jewelry always flashing
her inventory of precious gems
Gleaned from victorious liaisons

She'd bought her ticket
cross'd her fingers

How could she know
life's lottery
would come to this?

(At a 1999 Stroll of poets contest we were asked to write a poem using words from a long list. I chose these for the above and tied for 1st: misery, embroidery, comments, scandalous, responsible, dependable, glamorous, jewelry, inventory, victorious, lottery.)

In an intro to a book on the poet H.D. (Hilda Doolittle) we read "in her seventies she fell in love with Lionel Durand, a Haitian journalist....the pseudonym H.D. which had begun as her friend, Ezra Pound's invention, had transformed itself into the mirror image of D.H. Lawrence."

H.D. Was There

I know not what to do
I know she was there

I saw them in a doorway
(though this was but a dream)

She held hands with her lover
and I blinked awake

I lay on my bed
birdsong floating through muslin

and yet somehow she still stood
now seventy-five and more alive than ever

I had been dreaming of Hu
and the moon and shooting stars

and how they landed in the lake
without a splash I could see

how could I know this stranger
this old woman with her lover

a journalist he was
white teeth spotlighting shining brown

she was my lady of outrageous
my dowager of youth

my grandmother of life
my crone of possibilities

and I saw her with wild eyed Ezra
laughing hysterically

I saw her with D.H.
in the toolshed   Don't tell

and I saw her step forward
smiling to her lover

I saw the gardenia
he tucked in her white hair

I saw two pillows
two facing heads asleep

I saw her bent knees creaking
while she picked up a book

I saw her crooked smile
when their eyes met

and was it envy I felt
that morning

when birdsong through muslin
blew 'round me?

Today I Took My Daughter's Wedding and Engagement Rings to a Pawn Shop

        she couldn't
        asked could I
        love to
        wish she'd asked years ago

        scrubbed them with toothbrush
        and Arm & Hammer

        red neon flashed cash cash cash
        I swept past rows of guitars one tenor sax
        cameras carpets tea sets fern stands
        and cigarette scarred coffee tables

        cowboy buckled big gut pawnbroker
        took her blue velvet box
        squinted and with pointed pinkies
        delicately held rings in turn
        to light
        all his fingers gold encrusted
        knuckle dusted diamond chunked

        too bad no clarity papers he said
        and went behind a screen

I leaned on grazed glass counter over
rows and rows of other broken dreams
and wondered
do children pawn happy parents' rings
from fingers now dust

or were these like hers
wrong from the start
and worn too long
much too long

the pawnbroker rubbed red stubble
winked   handed me bills
red fifties
no receipt

Beginnings Again

Worth A Try

I'm packing for later in the senior's home
taking white cotton socks
without lumpy seams at the toe
the more expensive ones
not bought three per package
so they will fit under my new reeboks
with arch supports to help my knees
which seemed funny when
the arthritis doctor said it was worth a try
worth a try
I like that
worth a try
even when shy
like a father
unless he had a drink or two or three
blinking those light blue eyes
and the neighbour women or
mother's sisters would giggle
and say "Oh Bruce"
and he would say "Oh it's true"
and they would laugh again
and mother would look sideways
and ask him to lift the silver tea tray and then
"bring the dog in he's barking"
and I would be falling asleep
on the coral coloured chesterfield

wrapped in mohair hating when it touched my chin

and never thought what I would be when I grew up

I never thought

would I be my mother

or my father

or neither

or both

mother more likely to say

worth a try

my dad maybe

play it safe though he gambled

how could it be

a play-it-safe-gambler he bet sometimes across the board

maybe he wasn't a mathematical whiz

me too

my mother kept the books for her art club

no spreadsheets then

just a scribbler art gum and a yellow HB pencil

at the white enamel topped kitchen table

with the fridge its motor on top humming

the moon shining on poo-covered snow by the back door

our dog asleep in front of the gas radiant

my dad listening to Hockey Night in Canada with Foster Hewitt

and me cutting a paper doll

bending the tabs of her daisy

flowered dress with attached white frilled apron

over her breastless front

and talking for her as if she were a girl

who would give it a try

About the author

Bernard Wood

In 1934, six-year-old Joyce surprised family members at their usual after-Christmas-dinner concert by reading from a randomly selected section in the hefty Home Medical book in her grandfather Farrell's parlor. Her uncles had slept through piano selections and poetry recitations by older cousins but sat up when Joyce began to read. She sounded out the words phonetically as she had recently been taught. Her mother said "Thank you dear. Very good. That's enough." And Joyce received the biggest round of applause for her readings on the male reproductive system.

It was many years later that Joyce went on to write and read her own personal stories, some published in her first book *Girdles and Other Harnesses I Have Known* (Lone Pine Publishers, 2000) and now in *Twice in a Blue Moon* (Spotted Cow Press, 2007). She is a popular reader in Edmonton and surrounding areas going national with an interview on CBC with Michael Enright. The topic — Aging Dangerously.

Joyce turned twenty while on her honeymoon with Hu Harries. Together they had six children, losing their eldest, Tommy, in Edmonton's polio epidemic of 1953.

When Joyce was forty-five, her husband Hu, a Member of Parliament, was not re-elected to a second term of office as Prime Minister Trudeau's Liberals were wiped out in the West. But as an MP's wife, Joyce had dined with Elizabeth II, Queen of England and learned more than she had expected.

Joyce was widowed at fifty-eight; her beloved Hu dying of a massive heart attack while riding his horse in a competition. Joyce and a crowd of onlookers watched it happen.

Joyce began writing in 1996 and has become an active member of the Edmonton writing community. She is a member of the Writers' Union of Canada, the Canadian Authors' Association, the Writers' Guild of Alberta, the Stroll of Poets' Society in Edmonton and an associate member of the League of Canadian Poets. She has been active in her community through the years with the Junior League of Edmonton, IODE, the Edmonton Art Gallery, the Edmonton Youth Emergency Shelter and The Multiple Sclerosis Walk.

As the mother of six, and grandmother of seventeen, she has many wise observations which she shares with her readers in this book.